Mary Jane Reid
AΣX
140 West 5th
343-9500

One thousand years of drawing

Frontispiece
Fuseli *Man Embracing a Woman*
Black chalk
Kupferstichkabinett, Basel

Designed by Gillian Greenwood

Q. F. 18.

Anthony Bertram

One thousand years of drawing

a studio vista | dutton pictureback

General editor David Herbert

Note

The full names, dates and nationalities of
the artists are given in the index

© Anthony Bertram 1966
Reprinted 1969
Published in Great Britain by Studio Vista Limited
Blue Star House, Highgate Hill, London, N 19
and in the USA by E. P. Dutton and Co Inc
201 Park Avenue South, New York, NY 10003
Set in 8 pt Univers, 2 pts leaded
Made and printed in Great Britain by
Richard Clay (The Chaucer Press), Ltd, Bungay, Suffolk

SBN: 289 36916 9

Contents

Léger *Composition RUV* 1920
Pen
Kupferstichkabinett, Basel

Introduction

This book is an anthology of drawings arranged in groups to show parallel and contrast. They are all Western European and range in date through what, for simplicity, can be called a thousand years. They were not chosen for any art-historical reason but for their own sakes, for the pleasure and interest they evoke in themselves and in their interplay. The text is simply a running commentary. The groups are based on categories of representation, and I shall often comment on their quality as representation. In fact, unfashionably and for the sake of change, I am not considering art in the abstract and therefore not including a group of abstract drawings. Instead, I begin with a single example, which admirably illustrates Léger's pure and metallic intelligence, salute it, and then pass on.

It is difficult, perhaps impossible, to define just what a drawing is. The *Shorter Oxford English Dictionary* begins by defining it as 'representation by lines; delineation, as distinct from painting'. It goes on to a wider meaning, 'the arrangement of the lines which determine form . . . a delineation by pen, pencil or crayon'. Our first drawing is certainly in pen and it determines form, but not exclusively by delineation. Indeed, its character lies precisely in the interplay of lines and areas. But we habitually go a great deal farther than this: we accept as a drawing an artifact that has no lines at all—the one by Seurat on this page, for example. Such a work is a pure tonal construction and therefore, by accepting it, we rule out delineation as the specific quality of drawing. It so happens that both these drawings are in black and white, but a

Seurat *Au Concert Européen* 1887–8
Conté crayon
The Museum of Modern Art, New York (Lillie P. Bliss Collection)

great many others are in coloured chalks or in pen with washes of watercolour. In some extreme cases we accept as a drawing an artifact that is entirely in watercolour, such as the Constable on p. 73. Is a drawing, then, simply to be defined as an artifact in monochrome produced by pen or pencil, chalk or watercolour, but not by oil or tempera? That would seem very arbitrary. Who is going to exclude from the category of drawing an artifact in black ink with blue or brown washes? In short, how do we distinguish between a watercolour drawing and a watercolour painting? I think the distinction is this: where the forms in a watercolour are *constructed* in several colours, it becomes a painting. But by what term are we to distinguish a drawing constructed partly or wholly in tonal areas from one constructed primarily in line? I can think of nothing better than the awkward phrase 'painterly drawing'. This also implies the destruction of edges so that one form flows into another, and so produces an organic Baroque unity in place of the positive delineation of conceptual elements assembled into composition which characterized medieval and Renaissance art.

1 THE PERCEPT

Our groups of drawings fall into two broad categories. The first—the Percept—is concerned with objects perceived by the artist's eye, the second—the Concept—with objects conceived in his imagination. The distinction is not absolute and there must inevitably be some overlapping. In all concepts the artist must make use of percepts—if he conceives a human tree (p. 111), then he must also record his perception of a man and of a tree.

The exact nature of perception is highly controversial and quite beyond the range of this short book. It is the problem of knowing and seeing. We know that any object we look at is not really the shape of the object our eyes see. The known shape is inevitably distorted by linear perspective. The eye sees distant objects as smaller than we know them to be and often, through the action of aerial perspective, it sees them in colours which we know they would not have if they were near us. Finally, each one of us sees differently from the other and indeed we ourselves see differently in different moods or states of health. What our eyes register is therefore modified subjectively as well as by optical laws. The 'true' appearance of an object is an abstract conception: we *know* a square table but can never *see* one.

Heads and Hands

Most of the pictorial art of the world has depicted man, as if everybody had always known Pope's claim that he is the proper study of mankind. But man was, of course, most frequently used in early art as the image of God, of an invisible concept. I shall return to this later (p. 118); for the present we begin with man simply as an object to be drawn. Most early drawing, except for the illuminated manuscript, was primarily a means to an end; the study of elements which were to be used in a more durable form—in stone or bronze, mosaic, fresco or oil. Comparatively few such studies have survived from before the Renaissance. It was only then that they began to be seriously valued, and then largely by students and followers. It was they who preserved such studies as the one on p. 11 by Michelangelo. Although he must have been satisfied with the figure on the whole, since he followed it closely in the fresco, he was uneasy about some details. To the left he has redrawn the left arm, foreshortened. The head below it is closer to the fresco than the figure's, except that the

9

nose in the fresco is straighter than in either head here. None of the hands or feet quite satisfied him.

It is remarkable how often such studies fall into a composition, as if the creative artist cannot make any mark on a piece of paper without relating it to existing marks. Here, for example, there is a

Rubens *Studies for 'The Presentation in the Temple' c.* 1613
Black and white chalk on grey paper
Albertina, Vienna

Michelangelo *Studies for 'The Libyan Sibyl'* 1511–12
Red chalk
Metropolitan Museum of Art, New York

staccato rhythm of thrust and counterthrust, characteristic of
Michelangelo, which is in striking contrast with the ecstatic rising
spiral of the sheet by Rubens that faces it. These are studies for the
Presentation in the Temple, which is in Antwerp Cathedral. The
breathless exaltation of the heads, the sensitivity and tenderness
of the hands, are expressed in soft lines and passages of painterly
drawing that not only distinguish the two supreme masters but
also underline the difference between Renaissance and Baroque
drawing.

Picasso *Mother and Child* 1904
Black crayon
Fogg Art Museum, Cambridge, Mass

Leonardo da Vinci *Study of a Woman's Hands* 1478–80?
Silverpoint with white on pink paper
Royal Collection, Windsor
(reproduced by gracious permission of Her Majesty The Queen)

The drawing by Picasso on the left has the Rubens sensitivity and tenderness, but the sharper line and troubled staccato rhythm is closer to the Michelangelo. It is even more Mannerist, especially in the pervading emaciation and angularities. The contrast of the hands with Leonardo's is most revealing in this context. Leonardo has chosen long hands, but he has not elongated them; and he has been at pains to render their volume so that the eye does not run along them but explores their three dimensions. They were once thought to be studies for the *Mona Lisa*, but her hands are plump and these relatively bony; besides, they are much closer to the hands in the early *Annunciation* in the Uffizi, Florence. Although this drawing is in the dry and precise medium of silverpoint, these hands look soft and 'atmospheric' in contrast to Dürer's (below). Dürer's drawing, at first glance, we may take for no more than an exact record of what human hands look like, a masterpiece of emotionless skill. But this is wrong: the hands are as fully expressive as a Gothic spire. And as Gothic is a linear architecture, so this drawing is a piece of pure delineation. Yet it is far from pure outline. There is an outline, but within it the lines draw plastic forms. They also establish tonal areas, particularly through the contrast effected by the white lines. All these lines were painted with the point of a fine brush which seems to have caressed each rotundity and convexity as if Dürer, like a blind man, were feeling for the plastic form.

Dürer *Hands in Adoration* 1509
Brush point on blue paper, Albertina, Vienna

Grünewald *Man with Clasped Hands* 1522/3?
Black crayon, Kupferstichkabinett, Berlin

The hands in the Grünewald drawing above contrast strongly with Dürer's. They are fleshy and little articulated. Grünewald was not drawing the hands but their gesture, as part of the whole figure's gesture, the whole emotional concentration. The picture was probably a study for the St John in the *Crucifixion*, at Karlsruhe. His head strains upward, and this upward gaze, which we have already seen with a very different emotional content in the Rubens heads (p. 10), can also be compared with the drawing now attributed to Giovanni Bellini (below). Here, too, there is great suffering but with less questioning. The gaze is one of terrible acceptance. We do not know what it was intended for, perhaps Christ's head in an *Agony*; but certainly some part of a picture was started from it, because it is pricked for transfer.

The upcast look in Rubens's portrait of his son, Nicholas (opposite), has a very different effect. It expresses, I think, a great anxiety to please his wonderful father by sitting terribly still, and at the same time a childish embarrassment and boredom. I find

Giovanni Bellini *Head of a Man Looking Up*
Black chalk
British Museum, London

Rubens *Artist's Son Nicholas c.* 1625/6
Red, black and white chalk
Albertina, Vienna

it deeply moving when the most swagger of all artists turns away from his immense canvases to commune with a little boy on a piece of paper not a foot high. Such drawings of heads were commonly made in preparation for a painted portrait, but none exists to correspond with this one, or with the Holbein drawing

Holbein *Unknown Woman* before 1534
Coloured chalks and wash
Royal Collection, Windsor
(reproduced by gracious permission of Her Majesty The Queen)

Brancusi *Mlle Pogany* 1912
Pencil
Philadelphia Museum of Art (A. E. Gallatin Collection)

that we see opposite. This is very characteristic of Holbein's pure delineation, with the minimum of interior modelling, and yet the head is complete before us in its full volume. Behind the 'likeness', which is always convincing in his work, we sense Holbein's grasp of the essential structure, which the sculptor Brancusi brings forward with such emphasis (above) that we have no idea whether it is a 'likeness' or not. I do not even know, or much care, whether there was a real Mlle Pogany.

Van Eyck *Cardinal Albergati c.* 1431
Silverpoint
Kupferstichkabinett, Dresden

The sitters for the next two drawings are far from anonymous. Van Eyck's (above) was probably made when Cardinal Albergati passed through Bruges on his way to England as papal legate at the peace treaty between England, France and Burgundy in 1431. The portrait painted from it is in Vienna. Albergati was a most distinguished man, Procurator General of the strict Carthusian Order and Archbishop of Bologna. Van Eyck has superbly rendered the scholarly and contemplative but commanding face—a man, one feels, of austere self-discipline and compassionate justice. In the margin are Van Eyck's colour-notes, now mostly illegible. The minute precision of silverpoint in this portrait contrasts with the easy-flowing charcoal line of Dürer's *Maximilian* (opposite). This was apparently the only portrait Dürer made of the Emperor from life: it is the basis of his painted portraits in Vienna and Nuremberg, and of the large woodcut. The artist, in his usual methodical way, has annotated the drawing in the top right corner: 'This is the Emperor Maximilian whom I, Albrecht Dürer, drew at Augsburg in the Upper Palatinate in his small chamber in the year 1518 on the

Monday after St John the Baptist'. This *is* the Emperor Maximilian. We have a strong conviction that both these drawings are 'likenesses', whatever that may mean. They are certainly what the two men looked like to Van Eyck and Dürer on the particular days they drew them. We have no means of judging whether they would have looked like that to us. But there they are, there they exist, two men on two pieces of paper, as real as Hamlet or Mr Micawber. So it is with the next two drawings, two images of old

Dürer *The Emperor Maximilian I*
Charcoal with red, yellow and white
Albertina, Vienna

Andrea del Sarto *Head of an Old Man*
Black chalk
Uffizi, Florence

age. We do not know who Andrea del Sarto's old man was but
we do know what he is; it is all there in the free, excited black
chalk drawing by the artist who, of all Florentines, was nearest
to the painterly. His line does not so much define as evoke the

forms, and its weak, flaccid character exactly corresponds, one feels, to the old man's. There is none of this in Dürer's firm statement below, the clear factual image of decay and terror, as clear as his first written statement: 'This is Albrecht Dürer's mother. She was sixty-three years old.' And his second: 'And died in 1514 at the beginning of Rogation Week (Tuesday, 16 May) at two in the night.' Though the drawing was made before her death, it conveys his later description of it: 'She feared death much but she said that to come before God she did not fear. She died hard and I marked that she saw something dreadful because she asked for holy water, although she had not spoken for a long time. Immediately afterwards, her eyes closed. I saw also how Death smote her two great strokes to the heart.'

Dürer *The Artist's Mother* before 1514
Charcoal
Kupferstichkabinett, Berlin

Static Figures

The figure of each man or woman is unique, but the artist has, at different times and in different places, established his ideal man and woman. These ideals do not correspond to what we are pleased to call 'reality'. Blake said: 'All forms are Perfect in the Poet's Mind but these are not abstracted or compounded from Nature, but are from the Imagination.' These ideals, then, are the realities in stone or paint or pencil. How diverse they have been is admirably revealed in Sir Kenneth Clark's *The Nude* (John Murray Ltd, London 1956). The late Gothic drawing by Schongauer (opposite) illustrates the medieval ideal of elongation, in which the distance from a point between the breasts to the navel is twice as long as in the classical ideal. The Renaissance, of course, returned to the classical ideal and embodied it in the so-called Vitruvian Man. This derived from Vitruvius, the Roman architect who, writing in the late first century B.C., claimed that the ideal man, standing with arms and legs extended, fitted exactly into a circle or a square. Leonardo's statement on this is typical of the search for the ideal. 'If you open your legs so much as to decrease your height by $\frac{1}{14}$ and spread and raise your arms so that your middle fingers are on a level with the top of your head, you must know that the navel will be the centre of a circle of which the outspread limbs touch the circumference; and the space between the legs will form an equilateral triangle. The span of a man's outspread arms is equal to his height.' His version of the Vitruvian man (p. 27) is not a particularly pleasing drawing, but it does demonstrate these rather stocky proportions. Raphael followed them in his drawing of two nudes (p. 26), but he made a work of art rather than a theoretical diagram. Indeed, Raphael was not thinking theoretically but preparing for figures in the Vatican fresco of the *Battle of Ostia*. He was evidently pleased with the drawing, because he sent it to Dürer, who, as usual, documented it: 'Raphael of Urbino, who has been so highly esteemed by the Pope, made this drawing of the nude and sent it to Albrecht Dürer in Nuremberg to show him his hand.' According to Vasari, Dürer sent Raphael a self-portrait, a very characteristic thing for him to do. Certainly Raphael here shows his hand in the firmness and continuity of the outline and scholarly interior modelling.

Schongauer *A Foolish Virgin*
Pen and bistre
The Ashmolean Museum, Oxford

1515

Zafahell so bedig der so yet ycing yolt mach vt prait bit bi far wye hurteně bik avnacht vnd sar fil bin allwelt fine yny hewdeer zerfeler fo vny fand for lengig

Raphael *Two Standing Nudes* 1514/17
Red chalk
Albertina, Vienna

Leonardo da Vinci *The Vitruvian Man* before 1511
Pen
Accademia, Venice

Manet's study for *Olympia* (below) has the same type of outline, but it is more assertive and the interior modelling is less precise. In spite of this, the volumes are boldly established. The comparison with a recumbent figure by Rembrandt (opposite) fully demonstrates the vast difference between delineation and painterly drawing. Here even those elements which we might call lines are really narrow areas. Rembrandt has seen his object in terms of pure light and, instead of in any way defining it, he has created a new, equivalent object, which is the drawing. The heavy, dark areas in the lower left corner do not 'stand for' anything : they are their abstract selves.

This group concludes with three pairs of portrait-drawings with one by Ingres in each pair, to act as a touchstone. Ingres's obvious truth to nature is so astonishing that a superficial observer might accuse him of mere copying, but, in fact, he created symbols. He composed in lines, and there are no lines in nature. I

Manet *Study for 'Olympia'* 1863
Sanguine
Louvre, Paris

Rembrandt *Saskia Asleep* before 1642
Brush and wash
British Museum, London

could, of course, have said this much earlier; but there has been no occasion where the perfect impersonality of the line has been so completely fitted to an external personality. Ingres does not intervene. His line has a superb range of sensitivity—now firm and dark, now so faint that it barely reproduces. He and his line are always in the service of the drawing. It is not surprising that Delacroix spoke of him as absorbed in the ice of composition.

Rossetti, of course, was never frozen, but often over-heated. None of his paintings can be ranked with this drawing; perhaps because he could finish a drawing before the over-heating did damage. It remains, of course, a romantic drawing—it projects that image of his wife which he and his fellow Pre-Raphaelites had established. Years later Lady Burne-Jones described the memory of her: 'I see her in the little upstairs bedroom with its lattice window . . . and the mass of her beautiful deep-red hair . . . She wore her hair very loosely fastened up, so that it fell in soft heavy wings . . . the eyelids were deep . . . and had the peculiarity of seeming scarcely to veil the light in her eyes when she was looking down.' Rossetti has certainly drawn this, but was it the drawing and all the other images of Elizabeth Siddal that Lady Burne-Jones was remembering?

Ingres *M. Leblanc* 1823
Pencil
Cabinet des Dessins, Louvre, Paris

Rossetti *Elizabeth Siddal* 185(4?)
Pen
Victoria and Albert Museum, London.
Crown Copyright

Ingres *The Ladies Harriet and Caroline Montagu* 1815
Pencil
Collection The Earl of Sandwich, Hinchingbrooke

Our next Ingres, the superb *Ladies Montagu,* confronts a
Picasso (opposite) that was made at a period when he was
deeply under Ingres's influence, when in fact he out-Ingresed
Ingres. He achieved full plasticity with no tonal modelling whatso-

ever. This is surely one of the most economical drawings ever produced—mere outline has fully evoked the personalities and the three-dimensional forms. The hats sit on the solid heads with such an absolute quality that they become the images of abstractions, of silk-hattedness and bowler-hattedness. Finally, we

Picasso *Diaghilev and Selisburg* 1917
Pencil
Collection The Artist

Ingres *The Stamaty Family* 1818
Pencil
Cabinet des Dessins, Louvre, Paris

34

confront Ingres's *Stamaty Family* with Holbein's *Sir Thomas More and his Family*, the first a final statement, the second a study for a picture. Many studies also exist for Holbein's individual figures, but the final picture is now lost. This was the drawing which Sir Thomas sent to Erasmus, who wrote back that it was 'such a wonderful image of your whole family that I could not have seen you better if I had been with you'.

Ingres said: 'Draughtsmanship is the probity of art . . . Line drawing is everything.' Few of us will agree; but Ingres knew what he was up to. For him, for Holbein, for many other artists illustrated here, it was enough. The artist as critic is entitled to be on his own side, and probably it is better that he should be. That is why he is rarely a just critic.

Holbein *The Family of Sir Thomas More* 1527
Pen
Kupferstichkabinett, Basel

Figures in Action

There is a great difference between the depiction of a body in a position of movement and the evocation of the movement itself. I doubt whether the next three drawings can be claimed as in action at all. They really represent a transitional phase from our last group—they are figures pausing in action. In the first, the Mantegna below, we certainly experience a struggle of tensed muscles, an effort towards continuing a movement, but it is a kind of frozen movement which derives from Mantegna's obsession with classical sculpture. Indeed, I wonder if it is even a pause, whether the man will ever move again. He seems to be held rigid in the incisive and metallic line. The drawing has been related to Mantegna's *Dead Christ* at Milan, but this has been challenged on the grounds that the man is not dead. Yes, he is not dead; but the drawing has a monumental stillness which is like

Mantegna *Man Lying on a Stone Slab*
Pen and brown ink, British Museum, London

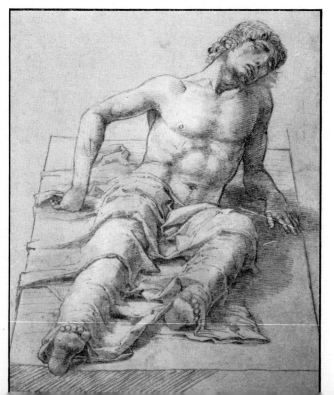

Primaticcio *Venus and Cupid c.* 1539–40
Red chalk, Cabinet des Dessins, Louvre, Paris

the stillness of death. In a remarkable parallel and contrast, Primaticcio's *Venus* (above) also raises herself from a recumbent position but with no muscular tension. Everywhere the eye follows the gracious and elegant outline. We at once recognize it as decorative. Venus certainly pauses, and so does Degas's *Dancer* (below). She stands vertically in a moment of balance which will be inevitably followed by some movement, some new relationship between legs, arms and body. I associate a fourth drawing with these—Pontormo's wonderful evocation of psychological action (opposite). Here, indeed, this master, one of the creators of Mannerism, profoundly disquiets us: here is some formidable disaster, some overwhelming question or denunciation. But is the figure actually in movement? Is it not merely tensed, like Man-

Degas *Dancer Adjusting Her Slipper*
Pencil and charcoal
Metropolitan Museum of Art, New York (H. O. Havemeyer Collection)

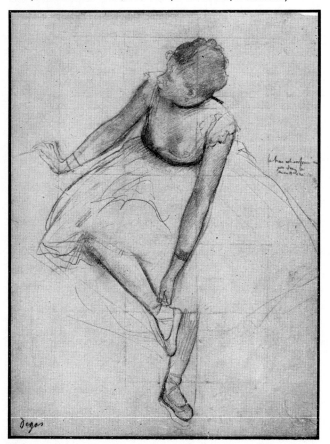

Pontormo *Nude Boy Seated*
Red chalk
Uffizi, Florence

tegna's? There is a difference; Pontormo's line itself seems to move. We can almost see his chalk sweeping and jabbing on its way. The extended arm and hand is like a bayonet assault, the lines of shading bristle. Here is a drawing that is itself active.

In the Tintoretto (below) which follows it, the subject and the line are both active. The action is free and the tension fully under the archer's and the artist's control—stress is resolved into harmony. This drawing is squared for enlargement, probably for a figure in

Tintoretto *Archer*
Charcoal with white on blue paper, Uffizi, Florence

Botticelli *Allegorical Figure*
Pen, British Museum, London

The Rape of Helen in Madrid. In contrast with the vigour of this and the Pontormo, Botticelli draws a lady—Abundance, Pomona, Autumn, or whatever she is—who only moves slightly, in a gentle floating sort of way. The lines of the drawing do their job of defining her body most satisfactorily, in so far as it need be defined for it is a most incorporeal affair, but they also move on their own as they swing and sway and curl about her.

Rembrandt *Old Man in Gesture of Welcome* 1629–30
Black-grey chalk
Kupferstichkabinett, Dresden

They do nothing of the sort in this Rembrandt—indeed, those lines which are structural hang heavily or curve so slowly that they cannot be felt to move. The large tonal areas hold the eye fixed on them. And yet, so wonderfully has Rembrandt conveyed the bowing gesture of the body and the welcoming gesture of the hands, that the movement of the whole man is unforgettably there. Rembrandt was one of the supreme Baroque draughtsmen, and he did not make line function for him in Botticelli's way. Neither did Rubens, though he obviously made a greater use of line. The eye does follow his outlines in the example here, but the essential movement is conveyed in the whirling volumes.

Rubens *Study for Mercury Descending*
Black and white chalk
Victoria and Albert Museum, London. Crown Copyright

Passing from single figures in action to groups, we find the first—the Pollaiuolo (below)—an excellent example of figures in positions of movement in a drawing that is itself static, a surprising thing in the work of a sculptor famous for his dynamic quality. These figures are as still as a row of Byzantine saints, though they resemble them in no other way. The lines define them, but have no life of their own. The subject of the drawing has never been successfully established, and no painting or relief has been found that corresponds to it; but it must have been a design for some decorative scheme. In contrast to this sharp arabesque, Renoir's nudes (p. 45 top) materialize like figures out of a mist. Their ostensible outlines are far too indefinite to define anything. The eye does not run round them, but embraces them in one untravelling glance. Here nobody is tugging at ropes or swinging swords, nobody is making even as much movement as Botticelli's allegorical lady, but the whole drawing moves like the sea. It is, of course, quite irrelevant that the utterly unclassical Renoir called this *The Judgement of Paris*. The women were all drawn from Gabrielle, the village girl, servant and model, who exactly filled his earthy and fleshly ideal. She could never have joined Bellange's ladies (p. 45 bottom), where long elegant lines sweep in parallel and emphasize the carriage of the bodies and their extreme Mannerist elongation. In the circular main group these lines surge upward and inward, and then farther upward and outward; it is their job to create these embracing organic forms.

Pollaiuolo *A Prisoner before a Judge*
Pen and brown ink, dark brown wash, British Museum, London

Renoir *The Judgement of Paris c.* 1908
Sanguine with white, The Phillips Collection, Washington

Bellange *A Gathering of Women*
Pen, Cabinet des Dessins, Louvre, Paris

Goya *Three Men Digging*
Brush and brown wash
Metropolitan Museum of Art, New York (Dick Fund)

Goya's three figures are also grouped in a circle—a quite shocking link, since otherwise the contrast is absolute. The drawing is called *Three Men Digging*, but is it nothing but a hole they are attacking with such battering fury? This is certainly the most triumphant rendering of violent movement we have yet seen. We should obviously expect to find such movement most conspicuously in drawings of combat, but I am not quite sure what is happening in the *Combat* of Cambiaso (opposite). This late sixteenth-century

Italian is little known as a painter but his block-drawings have recently attracted attention. Perhaps they are fancied as 'modern' and 'cubistic'. They are neither. Such studies were merely an easy way of establishing related volumes in clear defining lines and simplified areas of light and dark, in preparation for a normal Renaissance treatment in paint. But it does not seem that Cambiaso has stopped there. Certainly there is no continuity of move-

Cambiaso *Combat*
Pen and bistre
Uffizi, Florence

Raphael *Combat of Nude Men*
Red chalk
Ashmolean Museum, Oxford

48

ment here, but surely we do experience some kind of interrupted articulated movement. We can see at once that these cubic blocks are arbitrary in relation to any truly representational art, when we turn to the Raphael *Combat* (opposite).

It is common enough in his drawings to find similar underlying simplifications of forms, mostly into ovoids. In this drawing they are everywhere, and we shall see them again later (pp. 130, 131). They tend, I think, to interrupt the movement. In many places the eye at first follows round them, instead of pursuing a continuous direction. The great exception to this is in the right-hand figure and here, having felt its great sweep up and away to the right, we become aware of its relationship to the centre figure and then to the left one, so that suddenly the spray of three figures becomes quietly explosive. We cannot expect more violence from Raphael, the essential master of the High Renaissance—ever noble, serene and harmonious. Michelangelo was emphatically none of these things. He knew all about combats, for his whole life was one. The drawing below is the total image of violent movement; the very lines and areas clash and merge in the stress of conflict. Such a drawing evokes the drums and trumpets of Beethoven.

Michelangelo *Combat of Cavalry and Infantry c.* 1520
Pen
Ashmolean Museum, Oxford

Men and Animals

Uccello *Sir John Hawkwood* 1436
Silverpoint with white on *terra-verde* ground
Uffizi, Florence

Our next four drawings bridge the transition to animals, by showing them in relation to mankind. We begin with the horse which has so long worked for man, though it is not often depicted in its working life, as it is in Bruegel's drawing (below). This is itself a working drawing, as we know from the colour-notes and the inscription: 'from the life'. Bruegel's pen-strokes exactly convey the rough texture of the horses' ill-groomed coats and the peasants' clothes. This rarer view of the horse is at an extreme remove from Uccello's (opposite), where the horse becomes a movable throne, splendid in itself in order to make its rider splendid. The equestrian statue was the great prestige monument, and still is. Uccello has drawn such a monument for his fresco of the illustrious English *condottiere*, Sir John Hawkwood, which he painted on the walls of Florence cathedral. The drawing itself is in silverpoint, heightened with white, on a *terra-verde* ground and with a red background. It is squared for enlargement and transfer to the wall, but this will barely show in reproduction. This noble drawing, then, is proper to the horse in its proud and ritual function. There is another less stately but more triumphant type of equestrian monument—the conqueror on the prancing war-horse.

Pieter Bruegel the Elder *Peasant and Cart Horses*
Pen and brown ink over black chalk
Albertina, Vienna

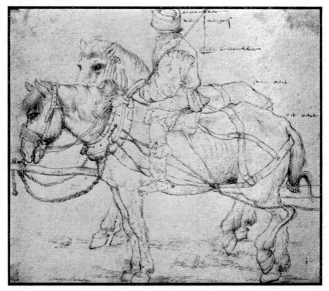

Titian *Rider and Fallen Enemy*
Charcoal with white on greenish paper, Staatliche Graphische Sammlung, Munich

To illustrate this we go from Uccello's finished drawing to Leonardo's working sketch (below), which is in fact unworkable. He made no provision for supporting the forelegs. The scribbles below indicate a prostrate figure holding off the hoofs with his shield. This was one of the first studies for the bronze monument to Ludovico Sforza, which was never cast. It is curious how emphatically linear the drawing is: Leonardo does not seem to have been thinking at all in three-dimensional terms. It is a lovely and lively drawing but it is no kind of practical study for a statue. Titian, handling a similar theme, has made a magnificent and triumphant drawing that was probably a study for a lost fresco. Its confident virtuosity and dash are so insistent that any further comment would be an impertinence.

Leonardo da Vinci *Nude on Horseback c.* 1485
Silverpoint
Royal Collection, Windsor
(reproduced by gracious permission of Her Majesty The Queen)

And so from the war-horse that 'saith among the trumpets, Ha, Ha; and smelleth the battle afar off', we descend to the horse considered anatomically, and to Stubbs. Such is the power of great draughtsmanship that, after a moment of deflation, we recognize that this, too, is a masterpiece. It is a statement of fact like a railway time-table, but it is in a different language. The abstract rhythm of the lines makes the difference. Having returned, then, to the horse simply as an animal, it is fitting that we have an illustration of the humblest, most domestic animal—the cow, that never 'saith Ha, Ha'. Cuyp seems to have loved cows. They are prominent in his landscapes, in the serenity of evening light. Cuyp drew this one as a study for such scenes. We can almost smell its breath. This is a masterly piece of observation, but it is more than that—it is drawn with love. Its great virtue is that it is not spoilt by anthropomorphic sentimentality. The cow is so humble that it is rarely seen as anything but itself. It is not heraldic.

But then, of course, even the lion need not be. Rembrandt's drawing (p. 57 bottom) shows no trace of the royal standard.

Stubbs *A Skinned Horse c.* 1776
Black chalk
Royal Academy of Arts, London

Cuyp *Resting Cow*
Chalk and brush
Musée Condé, Chantilly

Gaudier-Brzeska *Two Lionesses* before 1914
Pen
Victoria and Albert Museum, London. Crown Copyright

His is the natural beast as he himself must have seen it: the crouching, watchful pose is utterly convincing. His chalk must have moved with extreme rapidity to establish the main lines: the wash in indian ink may well have been added at home, and perhaps the more detailed treatment of texture in the head. In any case, the difference between this and the Rubens lioness above it is very striking. Rubens carried his much farther as a drawing: in fact, he made a complete picture, though it was probably a study for the *Daniel in the Lion's Den* formerly in the Duke of Hamilton's collection. Perhaps what gives it a slightly more heraldic look is that, although he drew many lions from life, he probably drew this lioness from a bronze in Padua. Gaudier-Brzeska's drawing (above) is very different, as unlike the Rubens as the Rembrandt—and yet all three are wonderfully like lionesses. During the years just before the First World War, this French sculptor spent much of his time at the London Zoo making these calligraphic outline drawings which are perhaps his best work. Here an extreme and sensitive economy tells us a great deal, particularly about movements—the loping, forward movement of the left lion, the turning head of the right. These beasts are as slow and cautious as the lines themselves.

Jacopo de' Barbari *Dead Grey Partridge*
Fine pen or brush point
British Museum, London

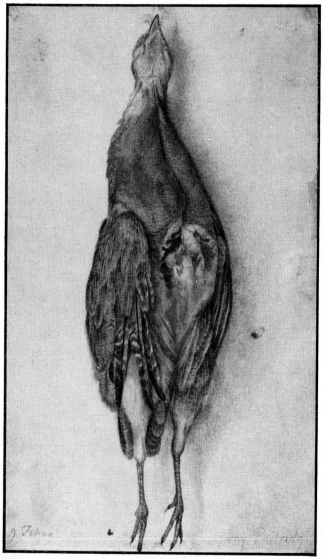

Giulio Romano *An Ostrich c.* 1524–7(?)
Pen and brown ink
British Museum, London

The last four animal drawings are of birds in outrageous contrast. The first (left) is dead, a grey partridge by Jacopo de' Barbari. Such minute and detailed realism comes oddly from an Italian, but we must remember that he spent many years in Germany and the Netherlands. The oddest thing is that his painting of a dead bird and a gauntlet in Munich was probably the first still-life ever painted. Though the grey partridge was a familiar and indigenous bird in Europe, an ostrich was probably a great rarity in the sixteenth century. This, and the manifest absurdity of the bird, must have attracted Giulio Romano; the Mannerists had a taste for the exotic, for anything that could surprise and shock. The ostrich is distinguished as being the only bird with two toes; there are three in the drawing above, but close examination of the original has shown that the third was added by somebody who thought Giulio Romano had made a mistake. It is, I think, a very nice ostrich, and it shows that however wildly imaginative Giulio could be, he could also be a close observer.

Tiepolo *An Eagle* 1750
Black chalk with white on blue-grey paper
Metropolitan Museum of Art, New York (Rogers Fund 1937)

From the dead partridge and the comic ostrich, we rise to the eagle, a heraldic and symbolic bird. Tiepolo's (above) was the study for the top of the herald's staff in his fresco of *The Marriage of Barbarossa* in the Bishop's Palace at Würzburg, and he has adapted the natural bird to its function. Its swinging buoyancy, its proud and conquering poise, bring us back into the poetry of Titian's exultant war-horse. Tiepolo has triumphed with the high rhetoric of his actual drawing. It is a most declamatory work.

Anonymous *The Planet Cygnus* from a twelfth-century manuscript (Harley 2506. Fol. 38)
British Museum, London

We end this group with an early drawing. It is an image of the constellation Cygnus from an early twelfth-century copy of a Carolingian manuscript, probably made in the Canterbury *Scriptorium*. The swan is remarkably accurate for a period when the exact observation of objects had not become a fetish in art. The astronomer may properly disparage the constellation, but that is a different matter: it is his business to be factual.

Landscape

Early artists were mostly indifferent to vegetable nature but
this attitude had been already modified by the thirteenth century.
Flowers were freely used to decorate manuscripts, and in such
themes as the *hortus conclusus*, the enclosed garden that symbolized the Virgin Mary. Little landscapes appeared through windows in countless scenes from her life and the life of Christ. These
uses were mostly by northern painters, such vegetable intrusion
being less acceptable in Italy except where the international
Gothic influence affected individual Italians. Michelangelo put no
flowers in his Garden of Eden, nor any other growth but the
necessary tree. Probably Altdorfer's *Landscape* in Munich was the
first pure landscape. That was in 1532. But others before him had
already shown a deepening interest in nature. Leonardo da Vinci
was certainly the most deeply curious and it is in every way proper
to look first at a drawing of his which reveals the very structure of
the earth, the skeleton which he here anatomizes. His pen, sharp
as a scalpel, reveals these stratifications but, since he was also an
artist, it goes off on its own, forming rhythmic curves and whorls

Leonardo da Vinci *Outcrop of Stratified Rock c.* 1510–13
Pen over chalk
Royal Collection, Windsor (reproduced by gracious permission of Her Majesty
The Queen)

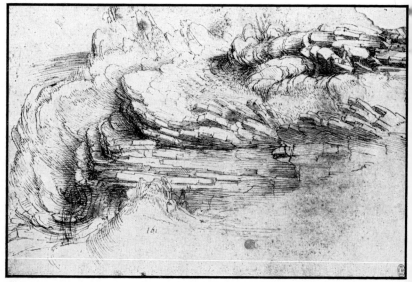

Cesare da Sesto *Study for a Tree*
Pen on blue-grey paper, Royal Collection, Windsor
(reproduced by gracious permission of Her Majesty The Queen)

that are pure expressive pattern-making. What is static to our short-lived eyes he has made dynamic, so that, for once, we seem to see the growth that fashions the rock. So in the study of a single tree, long attributed to Leonardo but now to Cesare da Sesto (above), the artist draws the rotundity of the trunk and branches, but in the firm continuity of his outline he makes the vertical movement dominate.

Claude *Trees in a Gale*
Black chalk with white
Ashmolean Museum, Oxford

Since trees are the noblest and grandest of vegetable growths, we consider them in four more illustrations, which fall into pairs. The first, the Claude (above), is of trees in the wind, so musically moved that they make it visible and audible. Claude has produced this effect almost entirely by the turn of the leaf, the flashing lightness that changes the whole look of certain trees when the undersides of the leaves are exposed. This is brilliantly done by the contrast of the opaque white with the black chalk. He has also used white for the sides of the trunks and branches and in the twigs on the extreme left. This has nothing to do with the turning of the leaves; it is pure 'poetic licence', which emphasizes that the wind comes from the left. De Gheyn, in contrast, has produced his effect entirely by directional lines, by the sweep to the left which shows that the wind comes from the right. He makes no use of tone and we are not surprised to learn that he was mainly an engraver and draughtsman.

De Gheyn *Trees in the Wind*
Pen on grey paper
Rijksmuseum, Amsterdam

Flinck *Landscape with a Withered Tree* 1642
Sepia brush
British Museum, London

Flinck was a seventeenth-century man and a pupil of Rembrandt's, and this drawing is characteristically Baroque and Rembrandtesque in the strong tonal contrasts and in the emotional choice of the old and dying tree. Its starkness against the white sky is a stroke of romantic drama which places him very exactly in his period. This, I think, is less marked in the companion drawing by Lievens, also closely associated with Rembrandt. He has not dramatized the decay of this old willow tree although, of course, his choice of such a theme is, to say the least, unclassical, since all decay, all imperfection, 'all things uncomely and broken, all things worn out and old' are, by definition, repellent to the classical mind and taste. But Lievens has relied a good deal more on line than one would have expected, particularly in the shoots at the top left and in the definition of the area just below them. His projection of 'mood' is less specific, less subjective, than Flinck's.

Lievens *Old Hollow Willow*
Pen with bistre wash, Kupferstichkabinett, Dresden

The famous phrase, originated by the nineteenth-century Swiss diarist Henri-Frédéric Amiel, that a landscape is a state of mind, is closely paralleled in Constable's: 'Painting is with me another name for feeling.' I do not think these statements can easily be disputed, but there is certainly some distinction between emotion served up hot and 'emotion recollected in tranquillity'. It would be too facile to say that this marks the distinction between the romantic and the classic attitude, especially when we recall that the last phrase is Wordsworth's—a romantic's. But we can perhaps use it profitably as a touchstone when comparing the eight land-scapes which follow. The first two are certainly tranquil. The width and depth of Cuyp's view (below), with no violent con-trasts, only the slow movement back from the dark foreground to the almost invisible hills, seems to be completely impersonal—

Cuyp *Dutch Landscape*
Black chalk and grey wash in foreground, coloured chalks in background
British Museum, London

a pure percept. And yet, after all, he chose it because he *felt* tranquil, as he did when he drew his cow (p. 55). This, too, is a state of mind; and he felt it in the presence of the object. Does the distinction, then, depend only on what state of mind is experienced? Canaletto's drawing, too, is still impersonal by the standard of high romanticism, but there is one marked difference. His style is more mannered and, especially in his curious system of pin-pointing, more personal. We are more conscious of the drawing than of the view. Is the distinction, then, one of style, because with a more personal style we *feel* the presence of the artist more sharply? But Canaletto does not normally strike us as a subjective type. Altdorfer does. While Canaletto was almost certainly studying a thing seen, I suspect that Altdorfer was probably composing a kind of thing seen, and very much through his own eyes. The

Canaletto *An Island in the Lagoon*
Pen and brown ink with grey wash
Ashmolean Museum, Oxford

Altdorfer *Alpine Landscape with Church* 1522
Pen and black ink with body colour
Boymans—Van Beuningen Museum, Rotterdam

romantic effect of his drawing here—I now allow myself the word
—is much enhanced by the colour. The clouds are in a sulphurous
yellow and in rose and violet, the clear sky is green-blue turning
reddish as it nears the ultramarine of the mountains. All the foreground is grey. The trees hang still in a breathless, almost sinister
pause. This is not tranquillity: it is emptiness and loneliness. We
70

shall see even more powerfully in Altdorfer's *Agony in the Garden* (p. 137) how he dramatized landscape. But his dramatization was less conscious than Brill's in the drawing below. This Antwerp artist had a foreigner's view of Italy. Though he spent most of his life there, it remained the young painter's Arcadia even when, in his old age, he made this drawing. It has all the characteristics of the picturesque and the sublime—the ruins, the waterfall, the grotto—which we associate with the second half of the eighteenth

Brill *Waterfall at Tivoli* 1606
Pen and ink with brown and blue wash, Rijksmuseum, Amsterdam

century. It is a more conventional romanticism than Altdorfer's and less deeply felt.

One of Brill's pupils, Agostino Tassi, was to become Claude's master. It is a paradox that Claude, the creator of classical landscape, also viewed Italy as a foreigner and in a most unclassical way. He wandered nostalgically among the ruins of Rome and in the Campagna in the golden light of evening and made those free, open, painterly sketches, such as our example below, which seem so remote from his formal paintings. They point straight to Constable and the Impressionists. And with this Constable that follows we may well ask not only: What has become of delineation but also what even of the trees and water? They are dissolved into a vision of light, almost an abstraction. It is a drawing so complete in itself that it hardly corresponds at all to the seen objects—the percepts—but becomes a direct expression of Constable's feelings.

Constable *Trees and Water on the Stour* (?) *c*. 1829
Sepia wash ▶
Victoria and Albert Museum, London. Crown Copyright

Claude *Tree and Hills*
Sepia wash
British Museum, London

We cannot speak of Claude's or Constable's drawings as distortions because they have wholly repudiated precisions of line: there is nothing to distort. But in this strange Bloemaert drawing of a footbridge the assertive line has an overall twisting, undulating action that does distort the normal representation of the object and reveals instead the concept of movement, and the action of time revealed within solids, as did Leonardo with the rocks (p. 62). But why should so commonplace an object be so agitated? The answer must obviously lie in Bloemaert's mood when he drew it. This manner was personal, but it was also of his time. He was a Dutch Mannerist of the late sixteenth and early seventeenth century. Van Gogh, 238 years after Bloemaert's death, made the drawing opposite in the Hôpital St Paul at Rémy, when he was in the deepest distress of his twisted spirit. It may indeed be a view of the hospital garden, but it is most certainly a view of that spirit. It *is* Van Gogh: the landscape has been metamorphosed, though not explicitly as in the Tchelitchew drawing (p. 111). We are at the extreme of subjectivism. The agitation affects everything, but in different ways to correspond with the character of the objective form. The trees writhe like blown flames. The distant fence conforms to its verticality in a series of straight jabs but the near one, being a hurdle, undulates. While charging the whole scene with his emotion, Van Gogh does still 'represent' the forms.

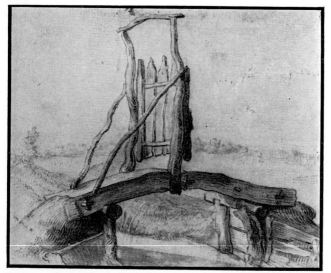

Van Gogh *A Garden at St Rémy* 1889
Reed pen
Tate Gallery, London

Bloemaert *Footbridge with Swing Gate*
Pen and ink with wash
Kupferstichkabinett, Berlin

If we look back at Claude's mountain (p. 72) and now at the one opposite, we can appreciate how Cézanne struggled to reconcile the painterly, in all its variations from late Titian to Van Gogh, with Renaissance definition and static composition—a reconciliation that also involved the romantic and classic, the subjective and objective. We remember his famous saying: 'I want to make of Impressionism something solid and durable like the art of the museums.' This drawing was made in the last year of his life, when the Montagne Ste Victoire, which he had known all his life, had become his major motif, his monument to the whole solid structure we call the earth, through which he revealed the permanence of being. His structural art of the museums, revealed in the painterly way of Impressionism, was ultimately a metaphysical statement. With Cézanne, landscape was raised to the status of religious art. He expelled all triviality of detail and only just suggested individual growth by the slight indications of trunks in the foreground, so unemphatic compared to Van Gogh's. The monumental stillness dominates. The theme is eternity.

This image of eternity is geometric. In a famous passage from *Philebus* (51, c.) Plato said: 'I do not mean by beauty of form such beauty as that of animals or pictures, which the many would suppose to be my meaning; but, says the argument, understand me to mean straight lines and circles, and the plane or solid figures which are formed out of them by turning-lathes and rulers and measurers of angles; for these I affirm to be not only relatively beautiful, like other things, but they are eternally and absolutely beautiful'. And to this we can add Cézanne's own hardly less famous pronouncement: 'Treat nature by the cylinder, the sphere, the cone, everything in proper perspective so that each side of an object or a plane is directed towards a central point. Lines parallel to the horizon give breadth, that is a section of nature, or, if you prefer, of the spectacle that the Pater Omnipotens Aeterne Deus spreads before our eyes.'

Cézanne *Montagne Ste Victoire* 1906
Watercolour
Tate Gallery, London

Saenredam *St Mary's Utrecht* 1636
Pen and ink with slight wash
Gemeente Archief, Utrecht

Architecture and Artifacts

Man-made objects have attracted artists less than animal and
vegetable nature, though they have played their limited parts in
most types of composition. The Haarlem painter, Pieter Saenredam, is one of the few important artists who have specialized in
portraits of architecture ; and he is the best. His preparatory drawings were based on elaborate diagrams and perspective projec-
tions, and were carried to a high degree of detail and finish, as we
can see in our examples. Most of his pictures were of churches,
generally of interiors. Their special quality is in their silent, serene
and noble evocation of space. We seem to stand alone in the
space and to experience architecture itself in a way that no other
pictorial artist achieves.

Saenredam *Utrecht Cathedral* 1636
Pen with wash
Gemeente Archief, Utrecht

Van der Heyden of Amsterdam also specialized in architecture between his early and later periods as a still-life painter. He also had a busy side-line as a designer of fire-engines, which no doubt attracted him to the subject of the illustration here. But in spite of this extraneous interest and the superficially ordinary statement, he produced a curiously moving work. We are startled and horrified by the burnt-out black windows, like empty eye-sockets. He may or may not have intended to stimulate this subjective reaction, but Piranesi, the author of our next drawing, certainly did. Even his 'straight' drawings were never such objective records as the three we have just seen. And when, as in our example, he was drawing his series of imaginary prisons, he indulged in the highest flights of subjectivity and romanticism. Here is a megalomaniac structure. The alarmed eye penetrates vast distances and mounts the dizzy succession of stairs and galleries to unknown heights. This prison does not threaten claustrophobia but the opposite—a complex of immense, uncontrollable spaces in which we lose our size, our way and ourselves.

◀ **Van der Heyden** *Burnt House in the Heeregracht*
Crayon, Stedlijk Museum Amsterdam

Piranesi *Interior of a Prison* 1744–5
Pen and brown ink with wash over black chalk
The National Galleries of Scotland, Edinburgh

It is a comfort to recover ourselves in the homely simplicity of Dufy's studio. Here are all manner of artifacts—pictures, chairs, tables, pots, brushes and bottles, and among them a comfortable lady reading the newspaper and a cat, as usual, resting. This delightful interior is not a mixture of life and still-life: it is *all* brought to life by the galvanic and embracing line.

Dufy *The Artist's Studio*
Brush and ink
Collection, The Museum of Modern Art, New York
(Gift of Mr and Mrs Peter A. Rübel)

Of all man's artifacts after his cathedrals and his homes, his ships are perhaps the most widely loved and admired. There were many excellent specialist marine artists in seventeenth-century Holland, including a whole family of van der Veldes. William the Younger was the best and most prolific. He and his father settled in London in 1672 and were the founders of the English school of marine artists—on the whole a much poorer product, for we do not label Turner by that limited title. But Turner was indeed a great lover of ships and of the sea, and he preferred it rough. His drawing opposite is one of several which he made after a stormy crossing to Calais in 1802. The contrast in the character of these two drawings is self-evident: it is the contrast between the unromantic Dutchman, who calmly sat under fire

Van der Velde *Battleships on a Clear Sea*
Chalk, pen and brown ink, grey wash
Staatliche Graphische Sammlung, Munich

Turner *Study of a Cutter* 1802
Black and white chalk on brown tinted paper
British Museum, London

drawing pictures of warships in battle or, as in our example,
showed them in their unheroic moments of rest; and Turner, the
high, excitable romantic, who invested even a little cutter with
dash and aplomb. She takes all the wind she can get and rides the
sea like a jockey.

In sudden contrast, after churches and prisons and ships, we come upon two farm-wagons. Such humble things were probably the least artistically valued of man's artifacts until very recent years, and even now they are mostly looked at and collected for archaeological and nostalgic reasons. Perhaps Rubens, when he made the study below, only thought of it as of possible use in a picture and indeed he did use the left wagon many years later in his *Return from Harvest* in the Pitti Palace, Florence. But however practical his first thought may have been, he drew the wagons with that particular intimate love he mostly reserved for the portraits of his family. It is a drawing of outstanding delicacy and lyricism. But the contrast between his great canvases and such a drawing is no greater than between Giulio Romano's flamboyant decoration of the Palazzo del Tè and his designs for goldsmiths' work. It is an admirable characteristic of drawings that they often reveal aspects of an artist that are not conspicuous, or even not present, in his paintings. Giulio Romano made many designs like the one opposite between 1524 and 1526. They are precise, careful and workmanlike. He was still, at that date, nearer to his master, Raphael, than to his own extravagances of the next decade. That accounts for the purity of line and harmony of form shown here, particularly in the jug. The last drawing in this group illustrates

Rubens *Two Farm Waggons c.* 1618–20
Black and white chalk, pen. Coloured chalks on sheaves
Kupferstichkabinett, Berlin

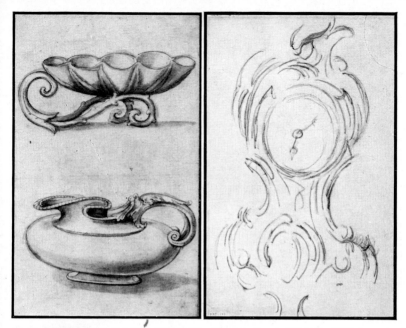

Giulio Romano *A Cup and Jug c.* 1524/7 (?)
Pen, brown ink and wash
British Museum, London

Cézanne *Rococo Clock* after 1885
Pencil
Kupferstichkabinett, Basel

the reverse process to Giulio Romano's. Here it was the artifact that sparked off the drawing. Cézanne had been exposed from childhood to, the Rococo of his native Aix-en-Provence. His early painting had been influenced by it, or rather, by the robuster and earlier forms of Baroque, but he had repudiated that for many years before the date of this drawing. When he made it, he was in the full flood of his research into three-dimensional forms, far closer to Poussin than to any Baroque artist; and yet here, at first glance, he seems to have transformed a solid clock into a flat curvilinear pattern of astonishing beauty and vitality. But we are struck by the contrast between the continuity and firmness of Giulio Romano's line and the broken painterliness of Cézanne's. Here we have the final paradox of a line that denies itself. And then we look again and pause and question. The lines vary greatly in their tonal value: the darker lines retreat: the ghost of the solid clock begins to assert itself. Its face advances and we suddenly feel that this is not after all only a flat curvilinear pattern.

87

2 THE CONCEPT

In this second part I shall largely leave the drawings as drawings to speak for themselves and comment rather on the iconographical aspects of the themes represented and on their relation to the imagination of the individual artist, and I shall say a little more about the artists. There has recently been a great revival of interest in the study of iconography, that is, of the meanings that are related to the image or symbol represented, as distinct from the artistic nature of the representation itself. This is of little concern in the case of such a straight forward subject as a kitchen with peasants playing cards in it (p. 92) or even an ambiguous subject like Sickert's (p. 95) ; but it is a very different matter where the subject is dependent on knowledge from outside the picture itself, as in the religious, mythological and allegorical subjects illustrated in most of our drawings from Picasso's *Guernica* (p. 104) to the end.

On pages 88–89
Bruegel *Summer*
Pen and brown ink
Kunsthalle, Hamburg

The Behaviour of Mankind

I have used this title because I include in this group a rather larger field than is usually understood by the word *genre*, which is so often limited to the domestic, generally peasant life of the seventeenth-century Netherlands. Such work passes no judgement on human behaviour, which is precisely what our later illustrations do. The drawing opposite is by Mathieu Le Nain, one of three brothers who were almost alone in practising *genre* in seventeenth-century France. Its French character is conspicuous in the classical and dignified restraint, which could be more easily related to Poussin than to the typical Netherlandish *genre* of the next two drawings.

90

Mathieu Le Nain *Two Peasant Women*
Red and black chalk, wash
Cabinet des Dessins, Louvre, Paris

The first is by the Haarlem painter Adriaen van Ostade, a pupil of Frans Hals. It is less coarse and boisterous than some of his work, but there it all is, the squalid and unpleasant aspect of truth that the pastoral and Arcadian poets and painters ignored. But the last drawing showed that it is not the whole truth about peasant life. The Dutch and Flemish *genre* artists seemed to prefer such aspects, like the recent kitchen-sink painters in England. The tattered quality of the drawing is exactly right for the theme. This has disappeared from the work of his pupil, Cornelis Bega (opposite). Simple family feeling is more suitably treated in a tidier technique. The drawing has been called a *Holy Family*, but surely even the least sensitive Dutch *genre* painter would not have introduced the background necking into such a subject. But we may well accept the holiness of the family, if we feel like it. Turning to Bruegel (pp. 88–89) from such minor artists, we are, in this drawing, confronted with an enigma. His attitude to peasant

Van Ostade *Farmhouse Kitchen with Peasants Playing Cards*
Pen and brown ink, grey wash
Ashmolean Museum, Oxford

Bega *Peasant Family*
Chalk
Albertina, Vienna

life was always ambiguous. He saw it from outside: sometimes
he enjoyed it as a comic phenomenon, sometimes he lashed it
with his fiercest satire. He was a moralist and much of his work
could have been properly included among the later drawings in
this group; but not, I think, this one. Here he seems to pass no
judgement, but he has certainly transcended mere *genre*. The
quality of earthiness remains but it has been transformed into an
image of man's triumph in the harvest. This is far from the pes-
simistic Bruegel who painted almost his last word on mankind in
the terrifying Naples painting of *The Blind Leading the Blind*.

There seems to have been no ambiguity in the attitude of Toulouse-Lautrec to his raffish subjects. This was the world he had moved into from the great château and the high lineage of his birth. These people amused him: they were picturesque, good-hearted and comic: he did not judge them. He was attached to none of the movements which agitated his contemporaries but projected his own matter in his own manner—a tragic and isolated genius who drank himself to death. An English contemporary, Walter Sickert, who outlived him for over forty years,

Toulouse-Lautrec *La Goulue et Valentin le Désossé*
Brush
Cabinet des Dessins, Louvre, Paris

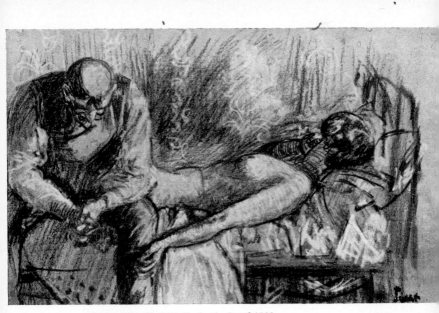

Sickert *What Shall We Do for the Rent?* 1909
Black and white chalk
Collection, Harry L. Dalton

shared his fascination with the world of popular entertainment but was even more attached to the drab lives of the lower middle-classes. He was a *genre* artist of the shady and shabby-genteel. *Genre* does not in its nature tell a story but a *genre* situation may easily suggest one. Sickert indulged in such stimulants with his tongue in his cheek. He first exhibited an oil version of this drawing with the title *The Camden Town Murder* and then he changed it to *What Shall we do for the Rent?* We do not need a very lively imagination to think of several other equally satisfactory titles. It is, one might say, a pregnant situation. But the drawing, as drawing, is simply *genre*.

In the next three drawings, all by Rembrandt, we move from this simplicity into the area of judgement. In the first, there is none. It is the record of a slight incident in everyday life, transformed by love into greatness. Rembrandt loved humanity in all its odd ways: he loved the child's exasperation, the mother's struggle, the old woman's faith in the power of a wagged finger, the onlookers' curiosity and entertainment. Here his pen was dipped in charity, but in the next drawing it was not: it was harsh and angular and critical. The pose of the man dictating his letter is dictatorial, the woman's is patient and submissive: that completes Rembrandt's parable. The next is Christ's parable, the *Prodigal Son*, a parable

Rembrandt *A Mother with a Stubborn Child* c. 1635
Pen and brush, dark brown. Black chalk
Kupferstichkabinett, Berlin

Rembrandt *A Man Dictating to a Scribe* 1648–50
Thick pen with bistre
Cabinet des Dessins, Louvre, Paris

Rembrandt *The Return of the Prodigal Son* 1635–42
Pen and wash with bistre, body white
Teylers Museum, Haarlem

of God's forgiving love. All human repentance and fatherly com-
passion and acceptance is in these few scratches of a pen and a
little bistre wash.

Rembrandt was not exactly a moralist. Though he observed and
recorded from a moral position, his moral remained implicit.
Hogarth's was usually only too explicit. It involved his telling a
story in a sequence of pictures. Since it would have been un-
balanced to have illustrated a whole sequence here, I chose two
drawings for one incident only in the series of engravings called

Hogarth *The Industrious Apprentice Performing the Duty of a Christian,* first
sketch 1747
Pen
British Museum, London

Industry and Idleness 'showing', as an advertisement explained, 'the advantage attending the former and the miserable effects of the latter'. Hogarth was a great *genre* painter, but he was a naïve and immoral moralist. The rewards and punishments he allotted were always worldly : honesty, for him, was no more than the best policy. His heaven was to be Sheriff of London. We can enjoy his art and yet judge his industrious apprentice to be a namby-pamby hypocrite and his future wife a simpering miss. Hogarth's judgement is not *in* his drawing.

Hogarth *The Industrious Apprentice Performing the Duty of a Christian,* finished drawing 1747
British Museum, London

Rowlandson's is. We could not differ from his judgement: the genius is palpably a ludicrous and pitiful fool who lives in the delusion that he is a universal man—painter and poet, musician and chemist, but not, I think, a master of domestic economy. Rowlandson did not measure his subjects as morally good or bad: he was simply amused, not angry. Daumier was. In his satirical

Rowlandson *The Chamber of Genius*
Pen and watercolour
Royal Collection, Windsor
(reproduced by gracious permission of Her Majesty The Queen)

drawings he was often very angry indeed. Lawyers were among his favourite targets. We need no story to understand his theme in this drawing: it is all in the counsel's hypocritical acting and the smug slyness of the guilty woman. With that look, she must be guilty. The comment of the public is gloomy indifference.

Daumier *Counsel for the Defence*
Pen and watercolour over black chalk
The Corcoran Gallery of Art, Washington (W. A. Clark Collection)

However angry Daumier might have been, he never reached the pitch of fury with which Grosz assailed the corrupt society of Germany and France in the years immediately following the First World War. This is not a drawing that needs iconographical explanation—Grosz has been brutally explicit. He meant to shock. His second drawing explains what had stoked his fury. Surely, of all man's behaviour, war is the most appropriate target for the moralist. But it was not war itself that Grosz attacked, so much as the activities of the safe civilian and the military machine behind the lines. The doctor proclaims the skeleton fit for active service— *kriegsverwendungfähig* (KV)—which the underlings accept as in the order of things and the senior officers find most amusing.

Grosz *Café* 1922
Dry brush and ink
Collection, The Museum of Modern Art, New York (Lillie P. Bliss Bequest)

Grosz *Fit for Active Service* (*Kriegsverwendungfähig-K V*) 1920
Pen, brush and indian ink
Collection, The Museum of Modern Art, New York (A. Conger Goodyear Fund)

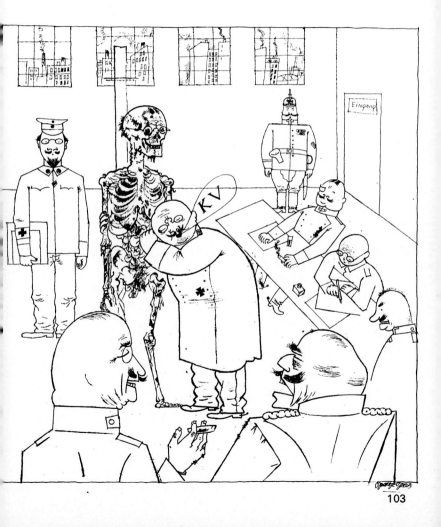

Picasso, a young and neutral Spaniard absorbed in his cubist experiments, was little affected by that war. He was profoundly affected by an incident in the Spanish Civil War, the bombing of Guernica, a small market town once the capital of the Basque people, by Nazi supporters of General Franco. This incident, trivial enough in world history, immediately became for Picasso a symbol of all brutal assaults by the strong on the weak. This he further symbolized in the theme of the bull as the destructive monster and the picador's horse as the helpless victim. He immediately began a series of studies, almost a hundred of them, for a vast picture which was to become perhaps the greatest work of modern art and among the most tremendous outcries against man's inhumanity ever painted. Our drawing is a study for the whole composition at one

Picasso *Study for Guernica* 1937
Pencil on gesso on wood
On extended loan from the artist to The Museum of Modern Art, New York

Moore *Woman Seated in the Underground* 1941
Crayon and wash
Tate Gallery, London

stage, but it does not include all the elements of the final work. The bull and the horse are there and the fallen man. There, too, is the ambiguous woman who lights the scene with her fragile candle—the light of truth and revelation, once a flaming torch in the more optimistic times of ancient symbolism.

There is no parallel to *Guernica*, but I have chosen to face it with a great contrasting work, one of the series which Henry Moore drew in the Underground stations of London during the war. Here is neither agitation nor violence but a monument of human patience and endurance, when each man and woman is alone and the future is a long grey tunnel leading nowhere.

Tiepolo *Zephyrus and Flora c.* 1757
Pen and bistre wash
The Barber Institute of Fine Arts, Birmingham University

Myth and Fantasy

Even in the Middle Ages, the classical myths were not entirely
forgotten. Dante, for example, made much use of them (*cf* pp.
152–157). From the early Renaissance to the end of the last
century they have served the painter in all sorts of ways, but
particularly in decorative painting. Our first drawing in this group
is Tiepolo's study for a ceiling decoration in the Palazzo Labia,
Venice, an occasion for the display of his masterly foreshortening.

Most of us will be indifferent to the news that the figures represent Zephyrus and Flora, who, in their turn, were personifications of the west wind and of flowers. The work of art remains valid though its subject now fails to interest us. Our only other example of classical myth is by Primaticcio, a pupil of Giulio Romano's, who went to France in 1532 and became the leading exponent of Fontainebleau Mannerism. Like his *Venus and Cupid* (p. 37), the drawing below was a design for the decorations there. It is filled with the typical haunting disquiet that we associate with all Mannerism. A question is posed: what are they all doing in their separate lives, these people who never look at one another, who move unaccountably, as if in a dream?

Primaticcio *Masquerade of Persepolis* 1541–5
Cabinet des Dessins, Louvre, Paris

Baldnung-Grien *Saturno* 1516
Black chalk
Albertina, Vienna

There could, one feels, suddenly start up in that ambiguous atmosphere Baldung-Grien's terrible, unambiguous head (above) that some later hand has called Saturn. The influence of Saturn was baleful and led in astrology to a sluggish, cold and gloomy temperament; but this is the face of active evil, fierce and merciless. Its squinting eyes see all the world as evil—its hair is blown about by the hot winds of hell. It is, quite simply, the devil. With this drawing and many that follow we must, if necessary, practise Coleridge's willing suspension of disbelief. We must accept, for example, the reality of witchcraft as an emanation from the depths of humanity. We can say that witches never existed, but we cannot say that man never believed they did. Man's belief remains a reality and Rosso represented it. That strange and disturbing artist, known also as Rosso Fiorentino, was one of the first Mannerists. The hysterical intensity of his foreground is accentuated by the quiet, classical background, where the wind of hell does not blow. The left, nearer witch brilliantly displays the attraction of the repulsive, the struggle between evil desire and fear. Here Rosso uses a horrid and splintered line.

Rosso *An Incantation c.* 1532–5
Pen and wash, École des Beaux Arts, Paris

Our next drawing is firmly attributed to Bosch in spite of the name Bruegel inscribed by a later hand. It is closely related to the *Hell* in his triptych called *The Garden of Delights*, now removed from the Escorial to the Prado in Madrid. We are accustomed to thinking of Bosch as a fantastic artist, perhaps the greatest, but we may be wrong. He was acquainted with a whole dictionary of

Bosch *The Human Tree*
Pen and brown ink, Albertina, Vienna

Tchelitchew *Tree into Hand and Foot* 1939
Watercolour and ink
Collection, The Museum of Modern Art, New York
(Mrs Simon Guggenheim Fund)

hermetic and alchemical symbols that most of us do not know, and the experts in these matters do not seem to agree very well in their interpretations. But the evidence is that he was clearly understood by his contemporaries and their immediate successors. Fray Joseph de Siquença, for example, an eminent Spanish theologian, wrote in 1605: 'His pictures are not drolleries but like books of great wisdom and art . . . a painted satire on the sin and instability of man.' It may be so, but certainly the effect on us is of a disturbing fantasy, and that is why the Surrealists enthroned him as a forerunner. In parallel and contrast to this, we can consider one of Tchelitchew's series of metamorphic drawings. This is obviously not composed on any systematic symbolism. It is a simple dream-image, familiar in folk and fairy tales. The artist has linked his vision to the whole mythology of trees

Fuseli *The Debutante* 1807
Pen and wash
Tate Gallery, London

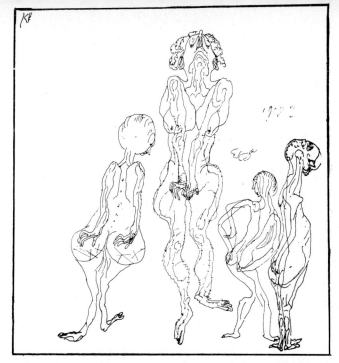

Klee *Four Nudes. Mother and Child Apprehensive over Father's Return* 1908
Pen, Collection, Lady Nika Hulton, London

The element of disquiet and ambiguity that occupies so big a space in fantastic art is excellently illustrated in Fuseli's *Debutante* (opposite). It is a drawing which can be 'explained' up to a point—the new girl is making her début in the brothel under the commanding eyes of the Madame and the leers of her new colleagues. Fuseli, by his title, compares her to the society girl entering the marriage market. But there are elements of profounder, less explicable, experience; and we ask questions: Is she sewing her shroud? At what immense distance is the monumental Madame staring? What is the half-barrier between the two parts of the drawing? Why is it that the débutante herself has witch's claws? How are we expected to respond to the girl who leers at *us*?

It is particularly disconcerting that we can also take such pictures as comic, like the Klee that follows, which was designed to illustrate Blosch's *Comic Epic*. But again we ask a disturbing question: what sort of life is led in that nude family which can produce such neurotic shudderings and distortions, such erotic squirms?

113

And so with the second Klee (below), *They're Biting*. This, too, is obviously comic, but we cannot fail to see that the fish in fact are not biting. They swim past the bait with an air of conscious indifference. And the exclamation mark asks the question: what on earth is going on? We are entertained by the comic uncertainties of men and fish, but we are also disquieted. Finally, in this

Klee *They're Biting* 1920
Pen and watercolour
Tate Gallery, London

context, there is Chirico's image of lost souls. The piazza of the little Italian town sleeps in the afternoon heat; the human beings are also asleep behind the shutters. But two beings hold a frigid dialogue full in the sun that they are too bloodless to feel. These are the robots, the men of measurements and straight lines, the computer-men.

Chirico *The Mathematicians* 1917
Pencil, The Museum of Modern Art, New York
(Gift of Mrs Stanley B. Resor)

The sequence of drawings we have been seeing reveals the worst aspects of humanity, culminating in the totally mechanistic, inhuman being. We finally escape from this into a fantasy of the best and least practical in man, embodied in the symbol called Don Quixote. It is not necessary to comment on one of the best-known books in the world; nor on Don Quixote's illusions, pictured by Goya (opposite), as he sits reading his books of knight-errantry. Nor is it necessary to explain the later stages, when the book has grown to a profound and universal criticism on all human life, and Don Quixote rides out with Sancho Panza. Daumier often returned to this subject of the quixotic man who, at the price of looking ridiculous, challenges the common man's prosaic world and is himself so innocent that he does not know that he is in fact ridiculous. Cervantes created a modern myth, which has more relevance for us today than Zephyrus and Flora.

Daumier *Don Quixote and Sancho Panza*
Black chalk and watercolour
Musée de Reims

Religion

The artist cannot represent the Deity. It may be symbolized by a circle or sphere, but even these abstractions are subject to limitations of space that are inconsistent with the higher concepts of Deity. It is possible in words to evade that difficulty to some extent, as in the famous definition of God as a sphere whose centre is everywhere and whose circumference is nowhere: but nobody can draw that. Since in Jewish and Christian belief (which is all that can concern us in an anthology confined to Western Europe in the last thousand years), man is the highest of God's creatures, and since God created man in his own likeness, man has no alternative but to depict God in man's likeness. In Christianity the problem is made easier because of the belief that

Anonymous *The Spirit Brooding on the Waters*, from an eleventh-century manuscript (Junius II, p. 6)
Bodleian Library, Oxford

Tiepolo *Angel on a Cloud*
Pen and wash
British Museum, London

God was incarnated in Christ; therefore an image of the body of Christ becomes relatively adequate as the image of his Godhead. Our first drawing in this group shows how this works. The unknown illuminator, probably of the Canterbury school and working in the early eleventh century, has used the circle as the symbol of Godhead and also of the round earth and of the circles of the heavens. The spiritual power is distributed through the agency of pure intelligences called angels. Since these have always been bodiless, the artist has used the image of a winged man—an image for such functionaries far older than Christianity. The mediator between heaven and earth is Christ, who descends to the earthly sphere and is identified in traditional iconography by his halo which contains a symbol of the Trinity and a reminder of the Cross. There is no modelling of the figures: they are insubstantial and weightless. It is interesting to compare them in this to Tiepolo's *Angel* (above), obviously another study for a ceiling decoration. In spite of the modelling, I feel this also to be a very insubstantial creature, so light, so delicate, so floating is it.

The problem of depicting religious ideas is even more acute than than that of depicting divine and sacred beings. The Psalms, for example, were rarely tackled satisfactorily. One of the most interesting exceptions was the Utrecht Psalter, a product of the School of Rheims made about 820. Later in the century it arrived in Canterbury, where three approximate copies were made. Our drawing is from the earliest and is dated about 1000 : it illustrates Psalm XXXVI in the Vulgate, XXXVII in the Authorized Version. There are no incidents to illustrate but with great ingenuity the illuminator illustrates the literary images. I can only indicate with verse references a few examples of how he went to work. Up the left side the mowing at hay harvest shows how the evil doers 'shall soon be cut down like the grass' (2) ; how 'the wicked have drawn out the sword, and have bent their bow' (14) ; how 'their

120

Anonymous *Psalm XXXVI*, from a manuscript of *c.* 1000
(Harley 603. Fol. 21)
British Museum, London

sword shall enter into their own heart' (15) as the wicked man
falls from where he was 'in great power, and spreading himself
like a great bay tree' (35). It is not difficult to identify the scenes
which show how 'the righteous shall inherit the land' (29) and be
fed (3) and satisfied in the days of famine (19) and their seed be
blessed (26). But this is not only a series of ingenious illustrations:
it is a revolutionary work of art. The Rheims illuminator and his
copyists discarded all traditional techniques and used a free,
broken line to sketch their vivid little scenes, a manner which was
to have far-reaching effects on drawing. It is an important distinction that whereas the original designer drew only in black,
his copyists drew in several colours, which by no means always
conformed to natural colouring. Tree trunks could be bright blue.
They were more interested in a rhythmic colour pattern.

Blake *The River of Life c.* 1800–10
Pen and watercolour
Tate Gallery, London

The Apocalypse or *Revelation* offers much more obvious op-
portunities to the visual artist, although much of St John's vision
is excessively difficult to depict. But rather than a depiction, I
have chosen Blake's personal development of the first two verses
of Chapter XXII: 'And he showed me a pure river of water of
life . . . on either side of the river was there the tree of life.' In
Blake's terms, these are Innocence on the left bank and Experience
on the right. In the right foreground Fate cuts the thread of life and
in the centre Christ leads the two dead children towards the sun,
the symbol of Deity. St John points to the river he has described.
122

Master of the Heures de Rohan *The Pool of Bethesda* before 1425
Ink with white on vellum
Herzog Anton Ulrich-Museum, Brunswick

The drawing above is attributed to an anonymous French illuminator known as the Master of the Heures de Rohan, and
dated to the early fifteenth century. Blake cannot have seen this:
the strange resemblances between the two drawings can only
suggest some very deep affinity between the two artists, both
concerned with watery themes. The Master's is taken from the
Gospel of St John (V 2–4). The sick lay round about the pool of
Bethesda in Jerusalem 'waiting for the moving of the water. For
an angel went down at a certain season into the pool, and troubled
the water: whosoever then first after the troubling of the water
stepped in was made whole of whatsoever disease he had.'

123

Palmer *Ruth Returned from Gleaning c.* 1829
Chalk and wash
Victoria and Albert Museum, London. Crown Copyright

We now begin a sequence of illustrations to events in the Bible and from the lives of the saints. The first of them is by Blake's youthful disciple, Samuel Palmer, and is taken in general feeling from the whole *Book of Ruth* but most specifically from the lines: 'So she gleaned in the field until even, and beat out that she had gleaned: and it was about an ephah of barley. And she took it up, and went into the city' (II 17–18) and the later return from gleaning when Boaz had filled her veil with six measures of barley (III 15). Palmer took this simple and moving story and wrapped it in the visionary glow, the magic and mystery of the 'Shoreham days', when he was one of the greatest poets among English painters, lifting the human body and all scenery to transcendent forms. The weight of that barley is the weight of grandeur. Altdorfer's *St Christopher* (opposite) is a striking parallel in the character of movement, the great staff, the swirl of the clothes and above all the solemn presence of a supernatural value. The mighty Christopher strides out through the water, ferrying a child, whose weight was so to increase that he could barely complete the crossing: it was Christ, of course, that he carried.

124

There are many biblical events which have not, in themselves,
any explicit religious connotations, such as the story of Judith and
Holofernes (*Judith* II 6 *et seq*). Judith was a Jewish widow living
in Bethulia when it was besieged by Nebuchadnezzar. She went
out to the enemy camp and succeeded by guile in penetrating to
the tent of the Assyrian general Holofernes. In his drunken sleep,
she decapitated him and returned to the city with his head as
evidence. Mantegna, in treating these themes, assimilated his work
to sculpture, drawing with a chiselled line as cold as marble. It is
magnificent but not war: Judith shows no more emotion than a
fastidious distaste. Classical restraint and objectivity triumph over
impassioned drama. Mantegna remains his austere Renaissance
self.

Rembrandt, on the other hand, was deeply involved in the humanity of biblical events. He felt deeply about the Flight into Egypt. He depicted Mary carrying her child and helped by Joseph, as she descended sadly to the donkey that was to take her to exile in Egypt. But I suspect that the drawing would be as wonderful and as moving if we knew nothing of the circumstance, as if Rembrandt had not believed the child was God. I must, however, emphasize that he did, that he was a deeply religious man. He frequently used supernatural lighting in his pictures but above all, I think, he tried to convey the humility of the incarnation. And he, in his own humility, drew and redrew the joined hands at the centre of his composition, the focus of his compassionate tenderness; and he also tried another position for Joseph's supporting arm.

Rembrandt *The Flight into Egypt c.* 1652–5 (detail)
Quill and reed pens
Kupferstichkabinett, Berlin

Raphael *Seated Virgin Reading to the Infant Christ* 1509–11
Pen and brown ink, Albertina, Vienna

This theme of human relationships in the Holy Family has most often taken the simple form of the *Madonna and Child*, with or without other figures. I have chosen to illustrate this with two similar studies by Raphael. The first was never used in a painting. It is a very free, linear design, a rapid jotting down of an idea that reveals Raphael's liveliness as a draughtsman. Two cherubs and a background are indicated with no determined shapes. Whirling lines in the foreground seem to have no other function than to create a rhythmic design. The second drawing is carried to its final state : it is squared for transfer to the famous canvas in the Louvre, Paris. But Raphael made many changes as he worked. His general tendency was away from the naturalistic elements towards the more perfect ideal harmony that is Raphael's music. In the painting, for example, while St John the Baptist still looks towards
130

Jesus, Jesus has turned his head up to his mother and she looks down to meet it. In the drawing, the relation of the two children is natural and well observed; in the painting it is suppressed in favour of a more continuous and ideally appropriate relation between the three of them. In the painting Jesus's head is above his left arm and the upward movement from his right foot is a continuous, gentle undulation. In short, the whole delightful effect of a child awkwardly and shyly peeping round its mother's knee is transformed into a nobler image. Much is lost, more gained.

Raphael Study for *La Belle Jardinière* 1507
Pen and brush, Louvre, Paris

We can associate those Raphaels with two other drawings of religious themes for known compositions. The first, the Carpaccio (below), is very close to the painting in S. Giorgio degli Schiavoni in Venice. Only details are missing, most conspicuously in the foreground. This is not a work of religious art, there is no trace of the sanctity of St Jerome: it is a *genre* drawing of an eminent sixteenth-century Venetian cleric and scholar at work in

Carpaccio *Study for 'St Jerome in his Study' c.* 1505
Pen and brush point in brown
British Museum, London

his library. The Rubens study for *The Last Communion of St Francis* in Antwerp is at the opposite extreme. Here is his first ardent vision of his theme, flashed down in vital, creative lines. The painting is tall and relatively narrow, and yet the general design of the actual communion is very close to this sketch. The principal change is that St Francis is brought forward into line with the kneeling friars in the foreground.

Rubens *Study for 'The Last Communion of St Francis'* 1618–19
Pen
Stedelijk Prentcabinett, Antwerp

There is little or no overt drama in the subjects of the religious drawings we have so far examined. There is plenty in the expulsion of Heliodorus from the Temple (opposite), which Delacroix has handled with all the vigour and magnificence of a great romantic. This is a manner which can be equally fitting to heroic secular themes. The theme, which even Raphael made dramatic in his Vatican fresco, is taken from the second book of *Macabees*, not now included in the Anglican Bible. Heliodorus, the prime minister of Seleucus Philopator, declared the treasure of the Jewish temple confiscate to the Seleucid treasury. When he tried to collect it, he was overthrown by two young men and a horse with a terrible rider, angelic defenders of the Jewish faith. This drawing, a masterpiece of dynamic draughtsmanship, established the design of the immense mural in St Suplice, Paris.

Delacroix *Study for 'Heliodorus Driven from the Temple by Angels'* 1857
Pencil
Collection G. Aubry

The remaining drawings in this group are related to the Passion and Resurrection of Christ. The passion is summarized in the widespread iconographic theme called *The Man of Sorrows*. Holbein the Younger treated it with a typically German emphasis on the ugliness of Christ's suffering as man, in the awkward, strained position of the body, the exhausted, almost unbearable face. He was just over twenty when he made this drawing and still working within the late Gothic tradition of his father. He was to repudiate it utterly in his later, more familiar work. Altdorfer, on the other hand, succeeded in reconciling this older tradition with the new German Renaissance outlook. In his *Agony* (opposite), he has dramatized the whole material world to a pitch that becomes

Holbein *The Man of Sorrows* 1519
Kupferstichkabinett, Berlin

Altdorfer *Christ's Agony in the Garden of Olives* 1509
Pen with white on reddish-brown paper
Kupferstichkabinett, Berlin

other-worldly. This is an exotic and fantastic garden, with no
trace of olive trees—a spiky and oppressed landscape that is fitted
to agony. Christ dominates in his isolation and in the symbolic
straight lines that occur nowhere else in the drawing. The dis-
position of the sleeping apostles is obviously borrowed from
Mantegna's *Agony* in the National Gallery, London. Altogether the
character of his drawing is derived to some extent from Mantegna,
transmitted through the Tyrolese painter, Michael Pacher; but it is
turned to a fundamentally different use. Mantegna was an Italian
classicist; Altdorfer, a German romantic. Dürer's signature and the
date in the right bottom corner are both false. The remarkable

drawing above is by Cranach, an earlier member of the Danube
school, who had a considerable influence on Altdorfer. It is an overwhelming image of total and flaccid collapse: it must surely represent the bad thief, because he is without dignity or hope.

The crucifixion of Christ was not depicted in early Christian art; and when it was first admitted, it was purely symbolic, an image of the triumphant redeemer, sometimes even robed and crowned, but never too obviously suffering. The realistic aspect only appeared gradually. I have not tried to illustrate extreme contrasts but to offer four examples for slighter and subtler comparison. The first (below) is by an anonymous illuminator of the late tenth century, and is from the Sherborne Pontifical, made there or in Canterbury for St Dunstan. Although it is purely linear in technique, it reveals the Anglo-Saxon artist's extraordinary capacity for suggesting the solid figure—as Ingres did. There is no sign of injury to Christ's body—neither the nails nor the wound in his side. God the Father is symbolized by the hand at the top; the redemption through the shedding of blood by the vase below, but there is no blood. Our Lady and St John do not grieve, nor do they stand on earth. They float, and their garments flutter weightlessly.

Cranach *Thief on the Cross* Chalk with white on red tinted paper Kupferstichkabinett, Berlin

Anonymous *Christ on the Cross*, from the Sherborne Pontifical 992–5 (MS. lat. 943. Fol. 4v.) Bibliothèque Nationale, Paris

Van der Goes *Christ on the Cross*
Pen with white on grey
Royal Collection, Windsor
(reproduced by gracious permission of Her Majesty The Queen)

Our second Crucifixion is by Hugo van der Goes, the fifteenth-
century Flemish painter who later became an Augustinian lay-
brother. It seems at first glance almost as serene as the last, but a
closer examination reveals certain qualities that belong to van der
Goes's abnormal sensitivity—the fear of hell that sent him mad.
There is, in fact, a subjective element. The figure is hopeless. The
face is pinched and poor and emptied of endurance, the limbs are

fragile and emptied of blood. The Dürer Crucifixion (below) offers a characteristic comparison. The body of his Christ is grave, noble, firm, upright and robust; his face troubled but not defeated. He stands on the ground. This is not, in fact, a Crucifixion but a drawing for one, made from a model—a humanist drawing.

Dürer *Christ on the Cross*
Pencil and white chalk
Louvre, Paris

Last and greatest of these four is Michelangelo's, one of those late drawings which were contemporary with the penitential poems. It was made under the stress of those years when he was struggling to disentangle himself from the world and draw closer to Christ. It is he, one feels, who clings to the cross in this unfinished, smudgy drawing that is a masterpiece of communion and communication. And for the same reason I have chosen him alone to represent the Resurrection. Here, in contrast, we are overwhelmed by the stupendous explosive uprush of Christ's return from death.

◀ **Michelangelo** *Christ on the Cross with the Virgin and St John c.* 1556–8
Black chalk, British Museum, London

Michelangelo *The Resurrection of Christ* 1532–3
Black chalk, British Museum, London

Bellange *The Three Marys at the Tomb*
Red chalk
Albertina, Vienna

144

To bring us down quietly from these summits, we close this group of religious themes with another Bellange (opposite). The three Marys stand by the empty tomb, so spiritualized that they show no violent human reaction to the miracle. They seem to glide, almost to float, so little emphasis is there on feet that tread the ground. The pure physical beauty of the drawing, the quiet mystification, act for us as the calm that follows the storm of the passion and conquest. We return to ourselves.

Dürer *Death as a King* 1505
Charcoal
British Museum, London

The End of Man

Dürer drew Death during a plague in Nuremberg—Death crowned as a king and inevitably triumphant, but exhausted by his excessive business. Death is pitiful. Then, on the opposite page, we see the death of man in its ugliest, most degraded form. There can be no doubt that Pisanello drew the hanging men 'from the life', perhaps as deliberate studies for his fresco of *St George* in St. Anastasia, Verona. He certainly used two of them. The two living figures he drew on the same sheet seem also to see Death—to obey Dürer's adjuration *Me(m)ento mei*. I feel that the grimness of this sheet is enhanced by the clarity and precision of the fine pen strokes.

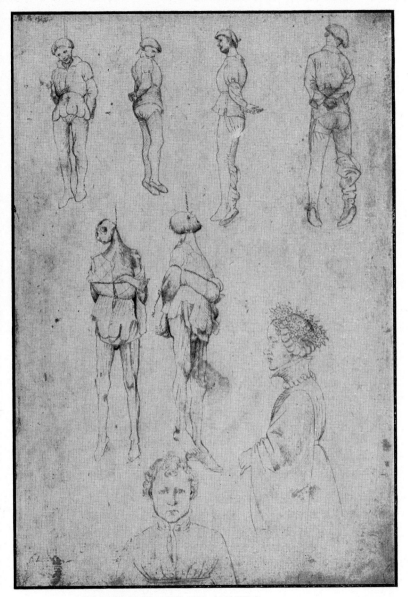

Pisanello *Studies of Men Hanging* 1437–8
Pen over black chalk
British Museum, London

Death reaped a considerable harvest in a plague, but man has long and often been haunted by the fear of a more universal death.

The greatest threat of it is today, but its greatest image is in the story of the Flood in *Genesis* (VI–VIII), though one remarkable drawing associated with it seems rather to be inspired by a passage in the gospels: 'For as in the days that were before the flood they were eating and drinking, marrying and giving in marriage, until the day that Noe entered into the ark, and knew not until the flood came and took them all away' (*Matthew* XXIV 38–9). Millais made this unfinished drawing (above) in the years before he perished as an artist in a flood of sentimental vulgarity. He was not concerned here with the Deluge itself, still less with its supernatural source. He pictured, with great skill and psychological insight, the reaction of different types to a catastrophic threat. So, we imagine, might we behave, each in his own way—some still wooing and eating, some understanding and some not. The invention is masterly. But Leonardo (opposite) looked upon the Deluge itself: he faced it out of what seems to have been an obsessive fear. In the later years of the fifteenth century there was

148

an outbreak of prophecies that the world would soon be destroyed by flood. The Church condemned this because of God's covenant with Noah: 'neither shall all flesh be cut off any more by the waters of a flood; neither shall there any more be a flood to destroy the earth' (*Genesis* IX 11). But all the same, the populace prepared for the disaster and Leonardo da Vinci, of all men, seems to have been deeply affected. In a succession of magnificent drawings he finally arrived at this stylized version. It was no longer a study of the pattern and power of water but of an irrestible, almost mechanical force. The 'waves' are like huge metallic dragons' tongues, and the square rocks leap and crash as destructive forces themselves rather than as the victims of the destructive force. Rain does not fall, but coils up like tongues. It is characteristic of Leonardo's complexity that in this tumult from the skies he has written an almost illegible scientific note on the nature of rain.

Leonardo da Vinci *A Deluge c.* 1516
Black chalk, brown and yellow ink
Royal Collection, Windsor
(reproduced by gracious permission of Her Majesty The Queen)

Michelangelo *Tityus* 1532
Black chalk
Royal Collection, Windsor
(reproduced by gracious permission of Her Majesty The Queen)

Michelangelo *Damned Soul* c. 1522
Black chalk ▶
Uffizi, Florence

And when man is dead, what then? Most of mankind has answered—hell or heaven. And most artists have found it easier to depict the punishments of hell than the rewards of heaven: they have had more models to work from. Happiness is difficult to depict, and the beatific vision is impossible. Michelangelo, for example, could draw his *Tityus* from a man and a bird, though Tityus, the son of Earth, was a giant whose body covered nine acres. His punishment for doing violence to Latona, the beloved of Zeus, was to be sent to Hades, where a vulture fed for ever on his entrails, which were for ever renewed. In this classical and finished drawing Michelangelo has not exploited the possibilities of terror. In his *Damned Soul* he has done this. He has made it all the more terrifying because we do not know what vision has started that scream in its whorl of lines like Leonardo's flood. This drawing was perhaps associated with Ariosto's *Orlando Furioso*, but more probably with Dante's *Inferno*. We know how profoundly Michelangelo loved and studied Dante, the poet who has inspired visual artists more than any other.

MICHELAN
BONAROTI
FECI: B
AT

Blake *Plutus* 1824–7
Pencil, pen and watercolour ▶
Tate Gallery, London

Blake, for example, undertook a complete illustration of the
whole poem, though he did not live to complete it. A hundred and
three drawings are known, mostly of the *Inferno*. One of the
finest is of Plutus, the bloated god of wealth and guardian of the
circle where misers and prodigals are punished (Canto VII).
Dante looks at him with apprehension but Virgil knows how to
silence his gibberish and he collapses 'like sails swollen in the
wind when the mast snaps'. Blake was not always so faithful to
the text: he often worked from Dante's vision into his own, and
even here his image of Plutus is identical with that of his Urizen.

At the beginning of Canto XXXI, Dante approached the lowest depths of hell, and through the murky atmosphere he saw what at first he took to be great towers but later found to be giants who stood on a ridge lower down in a deep pit so that only their upper parts were visible. Dante did not number them, but Blake made them five, to correspond with the five senses given over to materalism. The unfinished sketch of Dante and Virgil in the foreground establishes the scale of the giants.

I have set in contrast Botticelli's version of the same theme, but in a closer view (opposite). He also undertook a complete series of illustrations, one to each of the hundred cantos, and he almost certainly completed it, although eleven are missing. He followed

Blake *The Primeval Giants Sunk in the Soil* 1824–7
Pencil, black chalk, pen and watercolour
Tate Gallery, London

the text with precise fidelity. Here, for example, he individualized those giants that Dante described in detail: Nimrod with his horn, Ephialtes with his 'right arm pinioned behind and the other in front with a chain that held him girt from the neck down so that on the part of him exposed it was wound to the fifth coil', Antaeus who lifted the travellers in his hand and set them down in the depth of Cocytus. There, where the treacherous are locked in ice, Dante came upon two heads 'pressed so close together that they had the hair of their heads intermingled' and 'they butted together like two goats, such fury mastered them'. They were brothers who disputed their father's inheritance and killed each other.

Botticelli *The Primeval Giants* 1479 or later
Silverpoint finished in black and brown with brush
Kupferstichkabinett, Berlin

We see this incident in the background of Fuseli's drawing under the feet of the giants. In the foreground, Virgil has arrived at the heads of Ugolino and Ruggieri. Ugolino looks up from gnawing the head of his eternal companion. This is the most famous, the most devastating and the longest incident in the *Inferno* (XXXII 124–XXXIII 78). It is too compact to summarize: every word is vital.

Fuseli *Dante and Virgil on the Ice of Cocytus c.* 1774
Pen and ink wash
British Museum, London

Botticelli *Dante and Beatrice Ascend to Paradise* 1479 or later
Silverpoint finished in black and brown with brush
Kupferstichkabinett, Berlin

I have suggested why artists have mostly concentrated on subjects from the *Inferno*: this has been a great injustice to Dante. Dante wrote a comedy because, for those who are worthy, there is the way through Purgatory to Heaven. The meaning of the *Inferno* is only completed in the *Purgatorio* and the *Paradiso*. There, where most have failed, Botticelli almost succeeded—but only almost. The greatest poetry in Dante's final vision is out of the visual artist's reach. Here, in our last drawing, Botticelli has still some imagery that is amenable to representation. At the summit of the mountain of Purgatory is the earthly paradise and recovered innocence; and here Botticelli still has trees and water that he can draw. Dante has found and been forgiven by Beatrice and now, in this first Canto of the *Paradiso*, he rises with her into the supreme music of the final stage in his journey, where there is neither time nor space, an eternity which Botticelli drew as a circle.

Index of artists